TREMBLING HAND EQUILIBRIUM

Trembling Hand Equilibrium

BARRY SCHWABSKY

Black Square Editions

NEW YORK, NEW YORK 2015

COVER IMAGE: William Anastasi
Without Title (Walking Drawing: 10.20.08), 2008
Ink and pencil on paper, 7 1/4 x 11 1/2 inches

DESIGN: Shari DeGraw

ISBN: 978-0-9860050-5-3

BSE BOOKS ARE
DISTRIBUTED BY SPD:
Small Press Distribution
1341 Seventh Street
Berkeley, California 94710

1-800-869-7553
orders@spdbooks.org
www.spdbooks.org

CONTRIBUTIONS TO BSE
CAN BE MADE TO:
Off The Park Press
73 Fifth Avenue
New York, New York 10003

(*please specify your donation
is for Black Square Editions*)

TO CONTACT THE PRESS, PLEASE WRITE:
Black Square Editions
1200 Broadway, Suite 3c
New York, New York 10001

An independent subsidary of *Off The Park Press*

similmente operando a l'artista
ch'a l'abito de l'arte ha man che trema.

DANTE, *Paradiso* XIII 77-78

Contents

III QUESTIONS OF ART

IV KREDATI

Acknowledgements

Some of these poems have been published previously by the following print and online journals, blogs, and anthologies, sometimes in slightly different forms:

Bomb, The Bow-Wow Shop, The Brooklyn Rail, Colorado Review, Ekleksographia, Esopus, Fence, Fogged Clarity, Issue I, Marsh Hawk Review, NOON, Otoliths, P.F.S. Post, Shifter, Sous Rature. Truck, Vanitas, West Wind Review, With+Stand

Others were published in the print portfolios Gotham Haiku by KK Kozik (New York, VanDeb Editions, 2007) and Savage School Window Gallery by Cullinan Richards (London, 2008) and in the 2015 calendar A Poem a Day, published by Bruno Devos in collaboration with Curious, Belgium. 12 Abandoned Poems was published in a limited edition by Kilmog Press, Dunedin, New Zealand in 2010. Certain of the "[Unattributed Quotations on Drawing]" were first published in Mon Grand Récit: Not Every Fallen Leaf by Lee Bul (Seoul: Bartleby Bickle & Meursault, 2012). Many thanks to the editors of all those publications and to everyone else who cared to help these poems see the light of day.

I GATHERING DARKNESS

Abdul Wahid Khan was once asked why he limited himself to only two ragas, Todi and Darbari, which he practiced day in and day out. His response was that he would have dropped the second one too if morning time could last forever. One lifetime, according to him, was not enough to do justice to any raga. He was forced to change from Todi to something else only because of the setting sun and the gathering darkness.

SHEILA DHAR, *The Cooking of Music*

A Calm Death

Unlock my body
feed sleep some bitter fruit

let noon fix a seal
of wax on my head

the eye wanders
some call it homeless

a voice hears you
from mysterious places

the sun, a scratched lens
keeps leaning toward laughter

dropping crumbs of memory
the birds devour them.

Poetry Fell in Love with You for a Reason

Waking up nights: spare rooms crowded with heat
and the rain outside: sudden music for dull garden leaves
remember who's missing? and in the lightning of a smile
years of long kissing: a fantasy
sequentially yours: but even though you feel chosen

you are chosen: invisible difference
lasts long (this book smells like Murakami)
to an eye full of pauses: oily sky and goodbye.

False Positives

For once I died right
your host assimilating birds
a restless voice dims

backed off finding time
as if it were given me
to write it.

•

The great gray sea
the love engine chopped like mad
stand here totally reversed

but used to the filth of heat
this sky travels fast
knowing anyone else but you.

•

Again you close the door
a freezing whisper
and the room disappears

gulls fly past the pages
your eyes disguised
yet bid me enter.

Three Haiku for KK Kozik

Snow licks the window
Eyes cloud with memories – but
Oh! Feelings melt too.

Roses are threats;
And his love-offerings,
Never good enough.

Believe in love ghosts:
Every house gets the moon
It deserves.

Biopic (for Artie Gold or Syd Barrett)

A mind wrapped up around a sparrow's breath
or eye that wavers among branches

mistaken for a dragonfly
he knows music

has its cupboards where drugs
of solitude lay stored.

•

They found him painting songs
they couldn't hear

humming pictures they couldn't see
one about a girl with wooden hair

the ragged urban fox
free to let right go of itself.

•

He called her shadow
"my Saturday cinema"

well her shadow's more interesting
than she is, no?

whose finger reached
the whole way to the bone star.

•

"Marks scratched into the sky"
where a man disappeared

a relaxing thing would be painting
a white painting

but after microdermabrasion
the poem could well have stayed missing.

•

Go Venus, let's keep it legal
or dancing over dust she said

"You turn me out like a light"
but that was wrong

then buried her mouth in the flesh
of a peach imported from suspected sunshine.

A Fragment of Petrarch's Skull

I

Experts who specialise in the reconstruction of prehistoric human
remains exhumed the poet's skeleton this week in the village of
Arqua, near Padua. When Professor Vito Terribile Wiel Marin,
the paleopathologist in charge of the project, opened the marble
tomb he discovered that the poet's skull was smashed into
hundreds of pieces. The accident apparently happened in 1874,
the last time he was hauled out of his grave for inspection.
"We hope all the fragments are intact," Professor Marin said.
                      The Independent, November 20, 2003

I cry and reason between them
Where she who for test means love
And eyes its defense
When I blow moral reductions

For the mercy of its factor
Opened the way for the eyes
Coming in earth to illuminate the papers
Wave yes, beautiful Woman, to the world

I move the sighs to call you
The first sweet accents
Standard, the same voice, also
Sour fruit is picked

The throat and I sleep
Where the beautiful one dresses
Waves such similar fruit and is picked
Between the women a sun, in me, moving

Governments or turns, spring for me
Torsos of the true fireplace
To the shadow all nights are complained
And the loving looks in itself collected

It makes me frightening and slow
Between the other women
I turn to you
Behind every step with the tired body

It has its supplied age
For the extreme days of life, and how much more
Actions to twist me my fatal stars
The loving keys, the spirit exits

It does not come like coming
Nor wait for the light of this woman
In tenebrous places or late hours
To any animal it lodges in earth

When evening drives away the clear day
I aim cruel thoughtful stars
Made of sensible earth, and I curse
Lucent stars, volume down the loving forest

Yes, sweet dawn arrives
Still nearly in grass
It is written elsewhere
That in me that was not me seemed a miracle in other
    people

But the more I alter rivers
And already never then my language
Never in yes, sweet or yes, gentle hardenings
It opened the chest

The damage is yours
In front of eyes of dishonorable making
Great humid time I held
The ancient loads, calling dead women

Reductions in precious rain.

Scientists who have been examining what they thought were Petrarch's remains have discovered that the skull belongs to someone else. And they suspect it could be that of a woman.
The Guardian, April 6, 2004

Scarce
   beginning.
Lightning was
   smile-darkened
sky. Mother flesh experiments
   with an apple tree.

In doubtful sleep
   and long past thought
face the bed's last hour
   in weeping
silence vain. Scarce
   and teeming thought

my art once loosened
   dear time, cured
time of change,
   fattened up my peonies
until it hurt. I prefer
   the word "girlfriend"
to "lover" but I'm neither

and whose theory of poetry
    accounts for this,
the clotted rose? Whoever you are
    thank you. Burning clear
my fires kept hard
    like information shadows

a ghost community
    singing "Hell's on Fire."
Wandering Elizabethan in Chanel
    I'll write you a letter
suspending realism
    between desire and profit. Because

modern man seeks rent.
    The sun clanks along
color-cold but shadows promise
    waiting, a never-sung song
and if birth sounds dissolve
    that's poor tuning.

With shuddering storms
    sky grows serious.
In suitably bruised voice
    the numbers pour. I piss
on your plains
    in error

my dead thoughts ringing
    all over at once.
Use up language
    use it up I say
you need a muse of
    misunderstanding

with violence in her vowels
    sketched in umber on my ass —
wow, who'd have thought
    my little poem would come this far,
the lines stretch out this way
    to paint between things

but the clouds are with me
    as close as flesh is to thinking,
my refuge from the bees
    their power to hurt
she gave up in Tuscany to thrush
    my body, your naked brain.

Three Haiku for Lee Harwood

Orphan lines
Of verse in your wallet:
Ideal currency.

Two dark birds hover
Overcast sky hangs low
Past the clouds – who knows?

Pleasure spun backwards:
Words sticks to your fingers
You lick them slowly.

The Affirmed Life

Forget the taste slowly at first
not yours in tongue-tied longing

the pores of form
still drip with the sun's sweat

our eye companions
crowded in trembling doctrine

look past the keeper of geometries
address themselves to infinite understanding

spit mouthfuls of wasps
and cracked canary bones

yet uneaten by the whole of the page
an ache away from spoken dreams

they want to kiss your mouth dry.

Culprit

Our contact with the world is as direct
in vague thought as it is in any thought.
TIMOTHY WILLIAMSON

Accumulated delicacies
and laid at every table

emergency numbers, phenylethylamine
or whatever brings a fingertip into focus

fuzz like a ghost
you're maybe looking for

the last face abandoned
to create nothing out of something

we only dance and moan.

Children's Story

There is no satisfaction in telling a story
as it actually happened.

JORGE LUIS BORGES

Each house
has its over moon

repurposed by sleight of error
if not up in won't

our endless backlit something
forget poetry a minute

absolutely exposed
and was supposed to look but didn't

his voice an open vein.

Poem

Indestructible object
burnt in a fire of mind

a word said
touch untouchable distance

never really to be seen now
your eyes frost over

have we stopped hearing
eyes flicker in daylight

as good as gone.

Everything's Amanuensis

You always have to figure out what the line wants.
HENRI MATISSE

Listen you jerk
you can read that song

while seeing around
something lost in someone's eye

keep painting wet on wet
to cool in the shade of it

not too important to look
the past sings the present

some weary sky enables.

Falling Asleep at the Movies

Rain filled the 20th century
a piano burning and in the foreground
the radio set, the suicide cart
set some light in tatters

not as much fun for God
but at least can't you squint at it
the wrecker of cities flew in on waves of pictures
and noticed air molecules wandering

you know how those telephone poets coo
you said their names have no destination
and what is this strange sky
filled with armies of fireflies.

Bone Trouble

A shrinking whisper
come to collect your ashes

who used to be a sort of tube
of foil filled with memory

as through a distant city
some light would fail

the rubble of a fallen sky

fingers out through false colors
the dream he died to every day

and later buried
in the sleep of resistance

death is sticky with small flat feet
she'd thought of being stolen on his account

some daylight mad with love
wrapped it up in clear plastic

this way we are lived through.

Pure and Applied

Prospecting for air
or cheap memories of you

this unprotected death
preceded by its shadow

as if you didn't know
its hour passed hours ago

wrapped up in inventories
it sank into morning

on my agenda of expulsions
whose taste has been licensed

bright houses drawn
confirmed reports of breath

this fire eats fire
a future in which my fears are true.

Gathering Darkness

Hard to imagine but I never die
punitive starbursts last forever

the inattention of art
pulls mistakes from the depths of the sky

decoys of live birds tethered, blinded, or maimed
"What a dump!" in a voice over my shoulder

time ground down to sand
measure out a line as far

as its fate will go
truthless, tender

what wants to crash in the eyes of others
where otherwise would be nothing

spread the blood over my pulse
in your previously unpublished translation

how shadows flash past divination
if you only knew how haggard I was

a corpse dressed in honey
a corpse backed by birds.

II   12 ABANDONED POEMS

It is very foolish to hesitate between do and dew.

GERTRUDE STEIN

Poem

We're heading in the right direction. We don't know
what we're going to know but we'll open a bottle and taste
agave. Heading in the right direction: my latest
near-death experience, as a stand-alone
or as an add-on. In the right direction, fact fans:
seeing things and then getting wicked ideas. I'll top
whatever I see. The right direction: to live
to 80. I try and stretch all the time and do some sit-ups and
push-ups. Yeah well, if you're heading in the right direction:
We have more silence in our ears, a poem
I never knew was mine, loud songs
in memory of a hairline fracture. It better
have some pretty damn amazing gameplay. You're heading
in the right direction: getting into the meditative state as many
moments in the day as you can. Is this just madness? I don't know,
man! You're heading in the right direction so who am I
trying to protect? But don't forget
last night: I love the drama
of role playing. I'm a drama queen, and that's what
we do. It's like bottled liquid sunshine, and heading
in the right direction: my kids. I want the kids
to do what they truly want to do, but heading
in the right direction. We'll hold hands and never, ever
look back. I always mocked your game
because my whole game is speed, while yours
is obviously jumps and ramps. The right direction: where words

go missing. Sentences between leaves. Made-of things

won't hurt you. And one more thing, Batman, about what
we are trying to achieve, about us getting better. I'm doing
what I feel the need to do. Slim, lethal, the ghost
of an absence, you're heading in the right direction:
equality. If we're going to be equal, then let's all
be equal. New visitors forever, heading
in the right direction, despite rumors
the place was haunted: parents and animals.
It's a bit bitter. It was her long hands
I couldn't stop looking at. This is not about me being unhappy
with what I'm being paid. I signed a contract
and I'm going to live up to it. Everything I see or hear
reminds me of the poem I'm working on, reminds me
you're heading in the right direction. But I
figured something out for once: that heading
in the right direction, toward an inability
to see the universe, in all its glory, as a total accident
that came from nothingness all by itself: impossible.
I've got a pretty good work ethic, I can say. I will be fine
if I get a job but *totally not fine* if I don't. That
sucks. I need money, the source of most
of my problems. We lead symmetrical lives, both heading
in the right direction: live performance
as you can probably tell. The right

direction: the music. The live stuff, it sets me free. It's
that hour. We go up to the door. And in the right
direction: to avoid a violent confrontation. I'd rather
back off. Some guys'll grab hold of you and bust you up. So
I guess it's time for me to catch up with myself. Maybe I'm a bit
anxious, and my whole "deal" is paranoia, what's my bag
you ask? Well, all you cool cats promoting Bigfoot's existence,
fly away with me in the right direction: fishing slow
and just having confidence in what we're doing. We're kind of
the new kids on the block. These words in memory
of Electrelane, the only band we ever heard
in the last world. Goodbye. Okay okay – they're heading
in the right direction: "Fuck work" is the slogan
that started this company. It may not seem simple,
but practically, it is. I believe you should stick with the religion
you were born with. For me that's Judaism, and so that
is the only religion I'm against. The others don't even exist for me.
My photo shoot alter ago, you're heading in the right direction:
to get these guys paid. Then, I'll go back to the planet
where I came from. I feel kind of like I just
wasted a lot of time giving someone else pleasure but
we agreed to do this and we're doing it. With poppy seeds
between my teeth. You watch them slowly
and you're heading in the right direction: looking
for a good fuck. The next day I couldn't walk. Pop stars

for breakfast. The kiss that almost killed me. Well, in a way,
48   but not really, because of heading in the right direction: I never
even buy clothes because I get free clothes from all of my friends
who make clothes anyway. Whatever. Keep heading
in the right direction: promote tools that allow people to organize
and communicate in groups, particularly in local communities
around the world. I have no desire to be a pop
crossover artist. I wear a hat and I'm heading in the right
direction, playing my guitar. But I want to hear more hymns
that were done that way. To have my cadence considered
for centuries. Can anyone point me in the right direction?

After K. Silem Mohammad

Poem

To set this timber straight:
The eyelid of art shuts slowly
a tear keeps the orb from getting stuck
no punch lines. Genius loves conspiracy.

Mondrian straightens out his branches,
saying, "You've got to dream the lie
before you live it," then ducks
to avoid an oncoming sparrow.

"You've got to twist it to get it straight."
He's leaving all the lines but none
of the edges. Still the tree gets darker
at night so take your opportunity.

"Why date my works?" he keeps on thinking,
apropos of nothing. "I hardly feel I paint them."

After Geoffrey Young

Poem

Is this my last meal? Is this my only porn,
50   my only easel – my last sentence? Could it have been
floating in my head, flowing
into yours? The philosopher's
conquest: my only
look back, my only everything, except
yours the last whip and crack, my lethal
flight to quality, my low degree of bliss
overthought (were I ever to think again) –

My genius pants were far too tight.
They split under a cloud of images.
What cloud? Occulting what moon?
These are questions for aesthetic beginners.
"Tell us a secret," the piano sings,
immersed as it must be
in the language of the fathers, a cavity
as clean as the one we buried them in, long ago,
as soft as the hollowed roundness behind the picture plane
that slanted away that night, the aptly-shared intimacy we bent
on lovely knees, still shuddering
for art's sake and yet unwilling to burden time with poetry,
that night forgotten in your vaudeville life of silence.

After Amy King

Poem

The bloody show was entertaining us.
The poet runs from the stars.
The bloody show was causing us reaction.
Her feet, sublimely imperfect.
The bloody showy business made us money.
We use it to incite people.
The bloody business was a source of harmony
so we began collecting illness to spread
among us, the disciples of the bloody
cherry tree, our new name:
antibody.
Folded and kept in a pocket.
The business wasn't bloody; it was blood.
Blood, the pet name for a body.
A body gleaming sweat in headlights unzipped into mud.
Our open seams filled with sweaty words.
The rest of us zipped tight our skins and opened
an artery to the heart of my lover, leading right
through our enemy's, who did the bleeding for us.
Veins always bring the blood back in the right direction, don't they?

After Catherine Wagner

Poem

Grown obscure
among mortals

but plain
to the eyes of passing gods,

one with the night
condensing into mist

over water,
dispersed

with the first light
of morning.

After Kevin Killian (After Friedrich Hölderlin)

Poem

When a man has his tent ropes severed in sleep
so curling up on the cold earth to rest
the future is his only possible voice
the brief and fretted dream in which

arrested for treason having conspired
to seize so many stars he was presently silent
and slept in his secrets
but what may I ask ever happened to the sleep

he was buried in
was it not until evening
he heard your Highnesses' calls to account
he preached to Britain its manifest density

working upon their fears he persuaded them that
the accusation against Lord Russell was true
soon the letters swarmed across the page
like ants at a picnic

the Duke himself told them they were mistaken
but up he appeared in Westminster Hall
stars swarmed across the sky that night
my king he then died cheerfully in faith

passed gratefully into restfulness too
though the poem grew so long
sleep came upon him copying scrolls
amidst so many popping flashbulbs

what else can I say of his dreaming end?
he took his pipe out of his mouth when to sleep
his dream a stipend from some future time
and when the latter is said to be hard

lost his head and drank the warm milk
that the north shall come and he was told not to fear
for there was never any present tense
o heart of this love be the slave

fine sheets how soft how smooth
and after that the music unless we try
to stop it there is no turning back
until a man of skin

but look to the star that was written in an age
when sleep could make you happy
to stay in that island where they had landed
the falcon all the while rubbing its wings.

After K. Silem Mohammad (11)

Poem

A few go there

you ask me who but you know so well

and whose heart stopped

the pain a wasp feels when it stings you?

Don't stop at Deptford

don't blame it on my brown eyes blue

PVC harder-wearing than diamonds

lasts a thousand years

manufacture to landfill

Pegged together polyester blouse

odd sock, panties, woollen skirt

sour candy, bramble, ivy, marram grass:

Fragments from Gravesend

ghost memories, tricks.

After Simon Smith

Poem

Come police, arrest this night,

a perfume I take no pleasure in,

arrest this night in mythology becalmed,

distribution being its best

and only argument,

this pregnant night that lacks

the leaks to make it leaky,

arrest it in its calm evolution,

like asparagus in alkaline soil,

Martian perhaps, take it in for questioning

though in fact it may seem very friendly.

After Amy King (After Radiohead)

Poem

How many breathless

at the tiny golden flecks

like sunlight sticking onto my back & tongue finding love
    at the bottom of a bag

of personally-pan-fried parmesan & potato chips & fraught

with eyes wetting the grass

the sun made me hazy

knowing nothing of women

except in this poem & contented with shady places

death once removed,

fleeing all others, myself too

this woman alive showing in that view of me

the limestone flower

she comes always before me, a man befriended by

KFC boneless even on High Holy Days — a lover by name at least

nothing   less.

After Tim Atkins (After Petrarch)

Poem

Balocchi di grazia sì, fiori d'arancio
no.

AMELIA ROSSELLI

The isn't
division. Work ethic of hollyhocks,

indolent, redolent
counts as similar to this yard

Ah
the smell of you

is all you ever were
small girl biting

her way into a story
biting her way

through her soft yellow voice
to save what's worth saving:

bottom/lip/blood/red/sullied
under clouds

of paper. Any night
coming, I'll feel you

up and
right through that door.

After Louise Mathias

Poem

The poet no longer dreams of her coming breakfast. Inspiration
waits
in the caves at the heart of the mountain. She pulls the mountain
of heaven and earth around her but no longer sleeps
soundly. This routine is old. She's weary of the sublime hunger,
the swarms of melody, the eggs over easy.

After Robert Richman

Poem

You know this has all been done before
in the age of monster trucks
when shapes were as close as the objects of love
and their shadows would genuflect
as they backed off, a cause
from which language has resigned

                        you know
this has all been done as a formal reduction
with respect to the limits of the picture plane
– its unassuming spirit, inherently graceful
and I take great pleasure, however cheaply,
in it.

After Richard Hell

III   QUESTIONS OF ART

If, on a glass door, you see PULL written backwards, push.

UNATTRIBUTED

Playing Cards and Cigarettes

I would like to ask Basil King whether, when an artist paints the cards of the deck, one of them is a wild card. And if so which one? Furthermore I would ask what currency is being wagered in the game in which these cards are played.

I would like to ask Basil King about what happens when a *cohen*, a priest, becomes a *melech*, a king. Is that necessarily a promotion?

I would like to ask Basil King to recall for me the color of Franz Kline's bathrobe. I don't assume it was black and white.

I would like to ask Basil King if he knows the way from Alpha Road to Omega Boulevard.

I would like to ask Basil King if Klee and Ingres diverted themselves with the same fiddle.

I would like to ask Basil King where the hook goes when a question mark turns into a full stop. Does it then become the profile of an abstract portrait head?

I would like to ask Basil King whether, when reading his books, my feeling that I have read a given passage before means that I have really read it before or that I am only now, thanks to the grace of a second chance, able to read it for the first time.

I would like to ask Basil King if John Wieners looked any prettier in a dress than I think he did.

I would like to ask Basil King if an artist has subjects in the same sense that a monarch has subjects.

I would like to ask Basil King if learning to draw comes before drawing to learn.

I would like to as Basil King what rough magic turns painters into beasts and what spell it is that brings them back again.

I would like to ask Basil King if he ever thrashed it out with Joe Brainard about when and how illustration becomes a fine art. And how a book of memory becomes a text of the perpetual present.

I would like to ask Basil King how, when a man has lived many lives, read many books, and seen many pictures – how that man knows which of his memories are of what he's lived, of what he's read, of what he's seen.

I would like to ask Basil King whether Emily Carr and Virginia Woolf would have become lovers if they had met.

I would like to ask Basil King what playing cards and cigarettes have in common besides being sold in packs.

I would like to ask Basil King to explain the nature of prose incantation. Also, I am then led to wonder, would it ever make sense to speak of a painted incantation?

I would like to ask Basil King if he knows how it is that desire can outlive childhood.

I would like to ask Basil King how often a woman looks back at him when he looks in the mirror.

I would like to ask Basil King whether HD would have crossed the street to avoid WCW. Did she ever feel that he was stalking her? Would she ever have changed her routine, as WS (and I don't mean William Shakespeare) began to avoid walking through the village for fear that he might run into Baroness EF von L?

I would like to ask Basil King how to know when repetition is not compulsive but free.

I would like to ask Basil King how many times he has witnessed the death of a color. I would also like to know if he has ever seen one resurrected. Like certain flowers that faint away at a man's touch, then revive just as he starts to turn away.

I would like to ask Basil King whether he and Ronald Kitaj ever had a chance to wave to each other while crossing the Atlantic in opposite directions.

I would like to ask Basil King if he ever saw the movie in which Suzanne Valadon was played by Gloria Graham, opposite Humphrey Bogart in the role of Edgar Degas. I don't remember what it was called but it might have been directed by Nicholas Ray.

I would like to ask Basil King if what he found at the movies is what Pauline Kael lost.

I would like to ask Basil King this: "Sigmund Freud sees Egon Schiele / crossing the street" is the opening line of a joke, that's obvious, but is it what they mean by "Jewish humor"? And what's the punch line?

I would like to ask Basil King if he really remembers what yesterday smelled like.

I would like to ask Basil King to explain to me the difference between East London and Minsk, and whether that is the same question as, what is the distance between East London and Minsk.

I would like to ask Basil King if he knows, when the 1845 *Sunrise with Sea Monster* turned into the 1872 *Impression: Sunrise*, in the meantime, what had become of the sea monster?

[Unattributed Quotations on Drawing]

EDITOR'S NOTE: The following quotations were found written on notecards in a box on the desk of the late C.K. Rummage, Senior Lecturer in Drawing at the Slade School of Fine Art. The cards were written in a neat hand and the text of each was given in quotation marks, which we have reproduced here, but no indication of the sources was given for any of them. We present the texts in the order that cards were found in after the death of Professor Rummage.

"A drawing is the nervous system of an entity that does not yet otherwise exist."

"Certain drawings make you think of nothing but drawing; these are not necessarily the best ones, but they are the ones you may be least able to forget."

"All points are imaginary, and so are most lines."

"There are sketches for imaginary buildings, and a writer's notes may be sketches for an imaginary essay."

"A drawing is a conspiracy between the hand and the eye."

"Some drawings wear dark glasses."

"The hesitations that go to make up certainty reveal themselves in a line."

"Drawing happens when a pencil stumbles over a crack in the sidewalk while it's looking ahead at a point in the distance."

"To draw is a way of erasing the drawing you have in mind."

"When you see what it is a drawing of, you no longer see the drawing."

"It is possible to turn a sheet of paper inside out, isn't it?"

"A drawing is the future under a magnifying glass."

"But also, on paper, finished things can be disassembled."

"There are no more draftsmen in the world, thank goodness. Or hardly any, anyway."

"The marks are there to make the paper look good."

"They are merely trying to occur; they are checking whether the ground of reality can support them."

"A drawing is a conspiracy between the eye and the mind."

"You can taste a drawing: It is dry, but liquefies and becomes absorbable when you lick it with the tongue of your eye."

"A straight line vibrates."

"Ink is a liquid shadow; pencil, a dry shadow."

"Some painters who never draw (Caravaggio), many painters who draw incessantly (Menzel, de Kooning), but painters who draw just a little – none at all."

"If the paper is white, the line is backlit."

"Where two faces of a crystal meet: a contour."

"If you stumble while carrying a pile of drawings from one table to another, some of them may rustle in the air like startled pigeons."

"A single line is voluptuous but when they gather together, they grow grave and austere."

"What is more evanescent than a solid line?"

"A drawing is a window and also the breaking of the window."

"A sheet of paper is a kind of theater."

"The page is no longer opaque."

"Some drawings are woven by spiders to catch their prey in the finest, most delicate of filaments; others built out of sticks by birds to shelter their offspring."

"Information is not dependent on resemblance."

"The paper is there to make the marks look good."

"Either all lines are segments of one great line, or all lines are parallel and never meet, or both."

"A construction site on a Sunday, absolutely quiet. You can see all the equipment without hearing the din."

"Abstraction: a game. Representation: a double game. In certain drawings, where the choice seems to have been put off: rules are followed or violated at will. The game is itself in play."

"Conversations about drawing tend to trail off into incomprehensibility."

"Today, drawing seems to offer only two possibilities, both self-destructive: not to worry about being art or to worry about it excessively, playing hide-and-seek with itself."

"A drawing that looks you straight in the eye has something to hide, but the ones that try to slip your gaze – ah, they show you everything."

"Isn't 'finished drawing' a contradiction in terms?"

"The marks are there to make the idea seem plausible."

"One hand watches the other."

"If the eye is curved, then what do you mean by a plane?"

"When you roll up the paper, is the drawing still flat?"

"A sculpture can be translated into English, but a drawing into E-Prime."

"It's not necessarily the best artist who makes the best drawings."

"For the sculptor, drawing is a working vacation."

"You can't see it as well when you can only see it over the draftsman's shoulder."

"So to shadow as though it were not at all shadowed is best shadowed."

"A drawing without any shading is like a song without words."

"The idea is there to make the marks look necessary."

"If 'Venetian drawing' is a contradiction, is 'Florentine drawing' a redundancy?"

"Some drawings are answers without a question."

"There are drawings you keep trying to wake up from."

"To turn a crystal about in your hand, observing face after face, never being sure whether you are once again seeing the same face but from a slightly different angle, is already to have begun drawing it."

"How to make the paper push back?"

"No paper is so glossy that a line can slide across it without resistance."

"There are lines that do more harm than good, and vice versa."

"There are drawings that do more harm than good, and vice versa."

"Plato's great mistake was forgetting to exile the draftsman from his Republic."

"A drawing is a network, a multiplicity, and in principle should never be referred to in the singular."

"To assemble almost everything in almost nothing."

"There are drawings you have to calm down before you can look at them."

"'Opaque' and 'transparent' are words whose application to drawing is indeterminate."

"That some drawings are poems and others are recipes makes sense. What's strange is that the lyrical ones appeal to the sense of taste and the instructional ones to the imagination."

"It's not necessarily an artist who makes the best drawings."

"Taking with one hand and giving with the other. Taking with one eye and giving with the other."

"The teacher suggests drawing without lifting the pencil from the paper. Later you may notice that even when you have lifted the pencil, it is still in touch with the paper."

"A simple diagram may possess an involuntary eloquence."

"To draw a distinction twice has the same effect as drawing it once."

"To draw a distinction twice has the same effect as drawing it once, only more so."

"To draw a distinction twice has the same effect as drawing it once, only in a diluted manner."

"There are drawings with burning eyes, other blurred by their welling tears."

"On the scale of possibility, a drawing is larger than a monument."

"Sketch it when it is already perfected in your mind, and watch it dissolve."

"At times one is convinced that even fog has a crystalline structure."

"Just as you can draw a letter, you can write a picture."

"A line lags behind the hand that draws it."

"Is a drawing really always as good as it seems?"

"Drawings made by the blind as reminders to themselves for after the restoration of their eyesight."

"As digging tools go, a pencil can be better than shovel."

"I would like to ask Basil King if learning to draw comes before drawing to learn."

"Sometimes you have to be willing to play their game. But sometimes they are playing their game with you."

"The best part of a drawing is invisible."

"Drawing is for foxes. The hedgehog doesn't draw, only paints."

"If you don't know what a thing is, try to draw it, and see if it becomes something else, something you might now be able to identify."

"If the drawing fits the page, the page may be too large."

"A drawing is a difference of opinion between the eye and the mind."

"No statement concerning drawing is consistently true, including this one."

"There would be no drawing if the surface to be drawn on offered no resistance to the drawing implement."

"Wax crayon and thought on paper."

"Pencil and melted geometry on paper."

"Teeth-grinding and ink on paper."

"How to draw with a hammer."

"If a drawing falls to the floor in an empty studio, does it make a sound?"

"Did those who painted in the cave of Altamira make sketches beforehand?"

"The word 'humane' has never entered the vocabulary of drawing."

"A thought leaves a mark as evidence that it has been there. The mark provokes a thought that calls the evidence into question."

"If a statement could be true of drawing it would have to be true of everything else too."

"The best part of a drawing is what's already there."

"If a line marks the edge of something, what marks the edge of a line?"

"Drawing is a special mathematics in which one plus one equals three. Because if you have a surface (one) and add a mark (one more) you already have three: the two portions of the surface distinguished by the mark, plus the mark."

"I have seen drawings close their eyes in order to listen more intently."

"Black and white have no scent, but gray, yes."

"There is a drawing for the end of the world."

"Certain lines keep crossing back and forth, as if they'd forgotten something over there."

"A story can't be told but only retold and likewise a picture can't be drawn but only redrawn."

"Is 'drawing to a close' a contradiction in terms?"

"Not every drawing has a private life."

"This is an art for those who find the mechanism of an old watch more beautiful than its ornate casing."

"Some lines make, some lines mar, but no line does nothing."

"As I can learn to interpret your silence, I can learn to interpret your drawing."

"As with the ragas, some drawings are appropriate for morning, others for the hour of the setting sun."

"Drawing is a form of insomnia."

"Some drawings come with instructions for use, but most drawings need them."

"'Who is your drawing for?' Sometimes she knows who she is and sometimes she doesn't."

"It's so annoying when drawings complain about their neighbors. Why can't they all get along?"

"Tearing a photograph to bits is one way to make a drawing out of it."

"A drawing can be the seed of a painting in the way that an aphorism can be the seed of an essay or an observation the seed of a story."

"How big must a mark be to fill a page?"

"The most tenuous line cuts most sharply."

"The story behind a drawing is only its subtext."

"There are drawings played upon a flute, solo, but one scored for full orchestra, tubas and kettledrums included, is still a drawing."

"Some drawings seek and some drawings flee."

"Some artists draw the way some athletes practice. Other artists draw the way some athletes smoke."

"Some artists draw the way some writers read."

"A drawing is a difference of opinion between the hand and the eye."

"Some drawings are like prayers that you mumble in church on Sunday, others more like the one that might have been on the tip of your tongue as your car skids off the road and you see a concrete retaining wall coming at you. Try not to have to make either kind."

"Certain drawings are hot to the touch."

"There's something shady about half-tones."

"Do we ever grasp a form so vividly as when we feel it escaping our grasp?"

"...when impatience disciplines the line."

"Some marks are like excuses."

"Lines with a sense of touch or lines with a sense of sight?"

"... expansive brevity..."

"...to adumbrate the space in which the world can be reconfigured."

"When the line springs back into the page..."

"...melting into clarity..."

"...liquid wire..."

"...inscribed with a crystal."

IV   KREDATI

Kredati désigne le jeu des adultes, des enfants et des
animaux. Il s'applique plus spécialement à la gambade,
c'est-à-dire aux mouvements brusques et capricieux
provoqués par une surabondance de gaieté ou de vitalité.
Il s'emploie également pour les relations érotiques illicites,
pour le va-et-vient des vagues et pour toute chose qui
ondule au gré du vent.

ROGER CAILLOIS

Endless Remake

Our love is unanimous
like a piece of rotten prose
on the table, like some wild-ass
dove. Our love is hateful
and devoured, never mind
the change. As fast
as cash it helps keep
your eyes closed and then
a picture catches sight of me
and I am afraid of it. To keep
scaring the night just look
at our invincible distance.
Is resistance its own reward?
Stasis is as fast as we can go
and it sure is faster than cars.
Our images slink away.
Oops! This link appears
to be broken. Our glamour
can't survive here. I'll look
without knowing just who
is looking. Or else I'll be buried
in a modernist coffin
of luminous black
accompanied only by a young
and unlined notebook. I think

it's a girl. Our raging spirits,
our love against the wind.

Is a sparrow hawk apolitical?
Does its creaking
tear the sun? Abandon it.
Smash its voice
on the rocks
we took for monuments
and bring me its lonesome sound
in a jar. Our face dancing
leaves no record.
Bury the sun
in your chignon,
present your arms to me,
an excess of one
nascent
with excited colors
bent down in the gist
of spring. The silence
of a painting is not accidental.

Relapse

I can't stand to see your shadow
so switch my eyes off at dawn

to me these facts are mortal:
beauties twisted

to my will. They're singing
to the tune of your tears. The rest

is all difficulties. Return,
when you remember to,

my clothes, my face,
my voice.

The Sleep of Pictures

The sky looked in
from where my window had placed it
according to a timetable established
in all its murky charity
by the raining sound of cars

you can move your mouth across the image
on which a moth flutters
confused by the coffee on your breath
the stars are tidy in their places

but prefer to lean toward you
as if straining to hear a tremor
or ruffle the film of belief

that clings to our false memories of color
and the pleasures of nothing more to say.

The God Helmet

For Enid Baxter Blader

Your vowels are words under certain conditions

my eye pours its emptiness into them
and reads to the end of a distant word

my eye welcomes electromagnetic ghosts
just where I need them, just where belonging happens

the sun an Egyptian mirror and before that
undercoded with white dove frankness

before prophetic unfolding skin
declined in the name of science. I sit right down

and some pharmacists have said
our sounds come from clouds pumping blood.

Second Surprise of Love

– seeing thus
with stalking eyes
the laughter in her limbs
these fingers paint cornflower days white
but its gloss reflects the wrong face
you made a bad deal with music
it breaks your voice into bits of moisture
bright drops from a calm fountain
scattered
on the blind eye of a lens.

Utmost as a Stand

Calling
calling
a stand
horned and hornless
disgust

fine as a
           station
like a hungry bee
of wilderness

A child of epochs

an utmost play
to say an utmost hem.

Crossing

The light in her voice turned amber.

Soup with Landscape

1. Take one bag of parched birds
2. you know the ones I mean
3. tell your brain that
4. water pretends to fill the sky
5. sift ink through the glass transition
6. the ink used to paint this scene
7. should be generously diluted
8. then knead your argument with hypnosis
9. and absorbent stretched shadows
10. behind a sky held down with silver rivets
11. (Echo to Narcissus: What a baby you are)
12. roll out your drowned ballads with
13. statutory odors of rose water
14. a word alone and unread without blood sugars
15. effects of girls the morning fed us
16. whose doing things =; theater
17. now add the milk of branches
18. let age depletion feed my flesh
19. its colors sweetly stealing sea cream
20. say the taste of depends
21. and finish with a watery idea.

Ode to a Note as It Is Played Upon Your Lips

In a certain poem "The earth will
remember you" means "The sun
and moon will forget you." When
it submits in writing the words

"Your peace will linger endless as
the sea" it means "Your silence will be
momentary as the plash of a wave." One
leads to another and another leads

to none. A corpse is the loudest thing
in existence. Life teems so thick in it
though not its own that daylight
hides behind it, bogged down,

distracted from the smell of freshly
mown lawn. Utterance outruns
your geometric breathing and remembers
everything, *remembers* in the sense of *forgets*.

Utterance outruns. But I'll be
the one who trails behind you, silent.

Death's Widow

In rooms with running water
and peeling skin
she changed clothes
met death at the window
and sighed

her eyelashes slow
above a backmasked voice
complaining people don't stay put
no they never stay put.

Decus et Tutamen

Head wide under rusted flowers
can't commit but war may change your mind
love knows only love
so leave philosophy under the mattress

oxygen body, chemical music
or decomposition
so catch (as catch can)
the snow on your lip

an underlying grid structure: lace
in a station somewhere in the wilderness
years pass, too late for me
I heard its glow

sipped the milk of the instant
baby eyesore
calamitous sun
we should not abandon ourselves

collections of pearls, ashes, tears
of carnivorous paint
the gap between me and the air
the idea that eats us

intensified with my name
I'll send your little friends up
a voluntary accident
someone doesn't know as lettered coinage.

A Tour of the Horizon

What fault did the sky contain
at ease in its stench of broken colors
if not the sour gaze
of some face reconstructed by eye, not memory
an invitation to pay your rent, excessive

next thing you knew
I wandered lonely as a child
the printable day showed
silver maples with shadows of turpentine
poems that have fuzzy skin and appendages

yes, I feel sorry for your geometric breathing
your externalities, variances
they sulk feasibly in a fabled silence
where one leads to another
and another leads to none.

Charm Offensive

Come back, pitiless little corpse
to the frivolity of long-forgotten debates
this town's full of locavores so watch your step

accepting payments in kindness
my little heart-shaped mess
does not lack for translation, that is

this line could have been different
but why? just to show off its little difference?
probably half-dressed and pulling up its pants

or ashamed of this black silk whatsit
a placeholder redescribed as regifted
oh misunderstood sculpture longing to be consistent

in what it really is, nice try but
the ones that are not as bad
are not as good either.

Misnomer

nell'aldilà mi voglio divertire.
EUGENIO MONTALE

Whole
days
among the cliffs
more sensitive
than men of the world

listening
to extreme silence
split
my fingernails
or
darken, crack,
and weep tears of bitumen

and suppose
I'm not so tired
I won't try, won't fail
as lost
in the calculations
I didn't have
a dirty gradual
look

this weather leaks
as you sensed
shifting this
syllable
far to the right

you are the queen
of almost everyone
by day, by morning
by night in glycerin
you're watching
analgesic cinema
asking lots of breath
to share in the afterflesh
the earth is confusion.

Neither/Noir

Everything separating, falling
    away from itself
melancholy theme
    handled exuberantly
why? because coming apart
    is a way of hanging together

they coded from the heart
    but after their estrangement
in a number of oriental rugs
    we didn't know the music
flies to sugar water
    a rictus, a grin of sorts

and the darkness closed

in the absence of beginning
    a poisoning in the field
a beach taxi on fire
    hypersensitive
immersion into noise
    too early to be too late.

Little Synthpop Lullaby

A poem's lines are not in the order I wrote them
but in one that opens and closes
and divides itself invisibly

she told me dead leaves and frost make a slippery mix
you take the time to forget something
but not to step with care
or else pavement rises up to greet you

she told me
don't give away the beginning
just make a good enough murmur
to make your mouth taste different

in distaste for the sky
in love with all the music you hate.

The Dirt Project

The other you
whose imagery caws
these things we can't agree with
unfolds to the viewer
the true name of encounter
burning holes in the ceiling

a brief woman
caught me out of reach
with burnt leaves she put in her mouth
still open as usual
along with my cards I fold desire

thank you, the shadow banking system
considers you so obscene
making music just by talking
at the end of my mistakes
your ears want to take a breath

immaculate drudgery
a horizontal touch
the blade of music wiped clean
with words and all their opposites
the defenestration of color
to where things happens all at once.

Figure/Ground

Suspend caresses, drown ladders in slurry
these sign-objects ridiculing my efforts
or shrewd desire to capitulate
or recapitulate

confiding your heart to the clamor of pillows

that wasteful organ,
my joy is twisted
around
a solvent for loss

and plain as a pine coffin
our alibis crossed and got all tangled

look at the window – it's raining out.

Her Name Is Transparent

This false name is actually the name
only more irreverent than gentle
with the first and most conspicuous sign of said rumpling
the room is made dysfunctional, untidy

I like to point out that this voice is identifiable even in other
    places
I'd like for these to be references to her body more than to her
    biography
maybe another adjective suggests a continued drifting
a resistance to any fixed, final arrangement

does this name sound strange to you?
if so we can replace it by lurking
radioactive materials, smells or sound frequencies
some cool shit working even when almost completely hidden.

Felix and Dolores: A Short Novel

For Fani Papageorgiou

I

In this chapter we introduce our first character, Felix, a man
who never reads novels. For this reason, it goes without
saying, he will never become aware that he has been plucked
from the stream of life to be introduced into this narrative.
A man should read to improve himself, his situation in
life. This man is the hero of a tale in which he plays no
determinate part. On this particular early spring day the first
thing he does after walking out of his apartment – walking
out of his building rather – is to hold open to the sky an
empty envelope, letting it fill up with plump drops of New
York drizzle. He wants to mail them to someone as testimony
to the bond between his feelings and the objective facts of the
weather. Of course he knows the droplets will have dried up
long before the envelope reaches its addressee but also that
the drops will leave indelible marks, little puckerings of the
paper that will witness the former presence of its disappeared
contents. Paper has a good memory for water. Having
stamped, addressed, and mailed the envelope – we don't accept
his conceit that it should be referred to as a letter – he climbs
down the stairway at a nearby street corner and after a short
wait boards a Queensbound E train. He is not bound for
Queens. Stand clear of the closing doors please. Sitting there
lost in thought he does not realize that his mouth is hanging
open as his eyes scan the front and back of a newspaper being

read by the man across from him, who has a little tuft of hair blooming beneath his lower lip. Newspaper stories are not cluttered up with descriptions like the ones in novels. How had he gotten himself into this mess, he wondered. Some strange sort of hormone must be at work on his weathered old soul.

II

Originally her name was not going to be Dolores. But what else can I call the heroine of a story in which she plays no real part? She's only writing the story, or so she claims. But unlike her, others she knows (or can imagine she knows) – these others don't write. Some read. For instance the subway passenger over there reading a book called *Secrets of the Millionaire Mind*. Or they mail empty envelopes, not even fresh but obviously old and used, spattered with water. What kind of communication could such a person have in mind? It's like breathing into the phone as someone on the other end lets out a plaintive "Hello? Hello?" How much nicer to receive a simple postcard, perhaps one showing a bridge over a river in a foreign city or even the brilliant dust of a distant galaxy as seen through the giant telescope at an observatory somewhere in the clear-aired antipodes. "Wish you were here." Ha! The city itself, like the lens of this extraordinary and outdated instrument, is made of glass. It is a crystal with a hundred

thousand, a million, no, ten million facets. The problem, once
you start thinking about it, is to find the degree and angle
of light in which, as one turns the crystal over bit by bit in
one's mind, each one can shine. Spring mind, towering mist.
The train is never on time, only you can't really say that
because the train has no time. Or, as with the Queen of Hearts
(Disney's rather than Carroll's), all times are its times, all
time is its time, time times time is time, all time is untimed.
Perhaps this is what transatlantic travel was once like, for our
ancestors, the immigrants in steerage. It is their memory that
this chapter ends, now and forever, in false memory and in
disappearance from which recuse us, reader.

Barry Schwabsky's previous books include *Opera: Poems 1981-2002* (Meritage Press, 2003) and *Book Left Open in the Rain* (Black Square Editions/The Brooklyn Rail, 2009) as well as several works of art criticism. With the musician Marianne Nowottny he released the CD *A Voice Hears You from Mysterious Places* (Abaton Book Company, 2012). He lives in New York and is art critic for *The Nation*.

One thousand copies of *Trembling Hand Equilibrium* have been printed & bound at Thomson-Shore in Dexter, Michigan. The book is set in Rialto, a humanistic antiqua designed by Giovanni de Faccio and Lui Karner in 1999.